Winning The Scholarship

Race

Derrius Quarles

II

About the Author

Derrius L. Quarles is a student at Morehouse College and is a current Gates Millennium, Horatio Alger, Coca-Cola, Dell, Nordstrom and Chicago Scholar. During his high school tenure in Chicago, Illinois, Derrius accumulated over $1.1 million in scholarships. He is the first in his family to attend a four-year institution and is eager to help other students gain access to the resources that helped him get there. He has appeared on CNN, BET, and other media sources to share insight on his scholarship journey and has also been a guest writer for Scholarships.com.

With an intellectual enthusiasm for science, Derrius started performing research in 2008 as a Biochemistry Intern at Rush Medical Center where he studied the synthesis of polysaccharides in bovine spinal disk. He furthered his research experience at Northwestern University Feinberg School of Medicine as a Radiation Oncology intern, where he had the great opportunity of investigating the potential use of Titanium Dioxide Core-Shell nanoparticles as a cancer therapeutic. Derrius will enter the Boston University School of Medicine upon his graduation from Morehouse College in 2013.

Derrius is also the founder of DATA (Developing Access to Technology in America). Through this program, six students from Kenwood Academy High School have been awarded laptops, printers, and software to help them apply to college and gain financial aid. Derrius hopes to one day expand this program throughout Chicago Public Schools. In addition to science and writing, Derrius enjoys motivational speaking, traveling, cooking, trying new restaurants and foods, music, and photography.

CONNECT With MILLIONDOLLARSCHOLAR

Want updated information on The Scholarship Race and continued access to valuable scholarship resources?

- Connect on Facebook to stay updated regarding any speaking engagements/workshops near you in the future. Also, learn about current scholarship, internship, and professional opportunities for high school and college students.
- Connect via e-mail to ask a question about scholarships and to give book feedback.
- Use the upcoming MillionDollar$cholar website to download the MD$ Scholarship Pyramid™, the MD$ Scholarship Table™ Worksheet, activity résumé templates, and much more.

Facebook

www.facebook.com/milliondollarscholar

E-mail

info@milliondollarscholar.com

Website

www.milliondollarscholar.com (*Coming Soon*)

Acknowledgments

It would be nearly impossible to recall and thank every individual by name that has helped in some small way during my scholarship journey. So I will start by generally thanking all of the teachers, coaches, administrators, and mentors that have played a role in shaping my life.

To Mrs. Nuttaki, thank you for making science exciting, for recognizing my potential, and for not allowing me to give anything less than my best. Inez, thank you for introducing me to the world of financial aid; this journey truly started with you. Desmond, you were my first mentor in this journey; thank you for being the catalyst to my metamorphosis. Ms. Parker, thank you for the long hours, wise words, and great recommendations. Ms. Kirby, thank you for the opportunities, the space to grow, and the didactic scolding. Ms. Calloway, thank you for your encouragement that always kept my feet on the ground. Coach Roberts, thank you for working me so hard, and for telling me to make that first leap into the deep end. Lady Cherie, *pour me présenter au français, je vous remercie.* Ms. Stanton, thank you for pointing me toward the opportunities. Mr. Downing, you said Gates would happen first; thank you for all your help. Mzzzzz. Jackson, thank you for your help, guidance, and time. Dr. Easterly, thank you for inspiring me and keeping science alive at Kenwood. Ms. Sheth, thank you for all your help. Kendall, thank you for sharing your story. Mrs. Gordon, thank you for your time and advocacy. Mrs. Neely, thank you for all your help and for being there during times of distress. Mrs. Carter, thank you for all your time and care. Kevin Ladd, thank you for reaching out and sparking this project. Mary, thank you for your guidance and management. Abdi, thank you for creating the great artwork seen throughout this book. All the people at Chicago Scholars, thank you for your assistance. You were my very first scholarship organization, and your passions for building up students have shown me new possibilities and will continue to mold the future leaders of Chicago. To my extended families at the Coca-Cola Foundation, Gates Millennium Scholarship Program, Nordstrom, Horatio Alger, Dell, and Phi Beta Kappa Association of the Chicagoland Area, thank you for all of the guidance, support, and of course scholarship funding. To my fellow Chicago, Coca-Cola, Gates, and Horatio Alger Scholars, thank you for sharing your inspiring stories and for being such great friends. To my aunts and grandmother, thank you all for raising me and for being such strong, beautiful, and wise women. The journey has not been easy, but because of you, it has been fruitful, and for that I can never thank you enough. Lastly, I would like to thank God for sending every one of these people into my life at just the right time.

The world can be a cold place, so learn

how to make ice cream

CONTENTS

Introduction

Six years ago, while living in a foster home on the western outskirts of Chicago, the words *You ain't gon' be shit* pierced my ears on a warm summer day. I was thirteen years old then and was almost defeated. My foster mom had just told me I was not going to be anything in the future. I told myself to stand tall and not to cry, but I could not hold back the tears.

However, as soon as the tears started to come down my face—at the very moment I felt defeated—something amazing happened. I looked my foster mom in the eyes and yelled, "I'll show you! Whatever I become in the future, I know that I will not be like you." It was the first time I had ever stood up for myself—the first time I refused to accept defeat—and it felt great.

In hindsight, I realized that by saying that I would not be like my foster mom in the future, I meant that I would not beat up and discourage those in need of help. Rather, I would always empower people to fulfill their dreams.

Today, I am at Morehouse College on an all-expenses-paid scholarship. Not only do I have a merit scholarship, but I also accumulated over one million dollars in offered and accepted financial aid. ($1,145,000, to be exact.) This was the most financial aid awarded to a Chicago public high school student in 2009. After ABC 7 Chicago did a story on my scholarship journey, I was coined *"The Million Dollar Scholar."*

If I had the opportunity to sit down with my foster mom today, I would shake her hand and say *thank you*. I would tell her *thank you* because her words helped me realize that one day, I would be in a position to change the world in some small way. I would thank her because her words made me vow that I would always do my best to help others instead of taking advantage of them.

My journey to winning scholarships started long before my high school years. But at Kenwood Academy High School, I met the people who helped me gain the tools necessary to win scholarships. In this book, I will outline these tools and explain how to use them. I hope they can help you achieve your educational dreams.

During these rough economic times, scholarships are increasingly important because government-based financial aid options are diminishing while the cost of a post-secondary education is steadily increasing at a rate of about 5 percent annually. Not incurring heavy debt as an undergraduate student is a privilege, one that many students, unfortunately, never get to experience. After my success in earning financial aid, I found I was treated as an anomaly. I interpreted this in two ways: (1) earning over one million dollars in financial aid is an extremely special achievement, and (2) too few students are being taught the skills I learned in high school about how to win financial aid for college.

I believe the latter. Many students have access to a multitude of great resources, such as reference books and websites that list scholarship names, amounts, and deadlines. But these resources frequently lack the information students need to actually *win* scholarships. Though a list of scholarship

5

deadlines and amounts serves an important function, the list is somewhat **use**less unless you know how to **use** it. So instead of complaining about the wordy reference books and incomplete scholarship lists, I decided write this book to teach you the skills you need to win scholarships.

Helping students win scholarships is important to me because in my hometown of Chicago, I observed far too many high schools students with the credentials to get into college but no way to pay for it. Many of these students told themselves that could only apply to schools that have low enrollment costs, and in doing so sacrificed their ability to attend a better institution on the basis of their competitive test scores and grades.

Other students experienced what I call the "plight of the standardized test." In this situation, a student works hard throughout all four years of high school, participates in extra-curricular activities and community service, and maintains a competitive GPA, only to find that their score on a single four-hour achievement test has severely limited their ability to gain financial aid for their post-secondary education. These students begin to tell themselves that they will not be able to win scholarships because of their low test scores. But this is very far from the truth.

I have also observed students forced to work part-time during their high school career. These students often have lower grades because they had a difficult time balancing work and school, and they believe they cannot win scholarships because of their low grades. But this is also not true.

Other students believe they will never be able to afford college because of their home or family environment.

This book is for all those students. No matter what situation you face, no matter the financial aid hurdles you face, following the steps in this book can lead you to better outcomes in the process of applying for scholarships.

Students, I am here to tell you that you can do it: You can go to the college of your choice for *free*. I know it is possible because I did not have the best grades in my high school. The valedictorian of my high school class had a GPA almost a point higher than mine at the time I filled out the majority of my scholarship applications. I also did not have the highest overall standardized test score in my class (though it was a good score).

Don't get me wrong—grades and standardized test scores are important. Every student reading this book should strive to get the very best grades and score as high as possible on their standardized test(s). Be aware that both grades and test scores will be the very first criteria used to judge you during the scholarship application process. However, grades and test scores are not the end of your scholarship application. This is why I was able to win the most scholarship money in my high school class–and state–without having the highest grade point average or standardized test score in my class or state.

I came to understand and embrace the idea that the scholarship application process is like a race. Spectators and fans may believe that the racer with the most talent will automatically win the race. They may think that the quality of shoes will determine which racer wins. You on the other hand have to think differently. You are not a spectator or a fan, you are a racer; do not fall victim to a spectator's shortsighted perspective. Understand that in the race for scholarships, the racer who will finish ahead of the pack is the one that not only has talent, but also has a mind focused on winning and the preparation necessary to win. You have to know that the quality of shoes will have nothing to do with which racer wins race, its what the racer does in the shoes that matters.

If you want to be a winner, you cannot rely on your talent; you have to develop every component that goes into being a great competitor in the race. This book, along with your willingness to work hard, will help you to become that student who crosses the finish line first in the race for scholarships.

THE $CHOLARSHIP STATE OF MIND

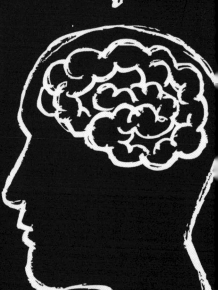

Want to know the most interesting thing about scholarship applications? The most important part of the application is not a part of the application at all. Sounds weird right? Well, it is somewhat weird, and in order to win scholarships, you are going to have to become a little bit weird in your way of thinking. Before you pick up any scholarship applications, before you write any personal statements, and before you do anything related to scholarships, you are going to have to do something out of the ordinary and unusual: You have to develop what I call The $cholarship State of Mind. It is the first and the most important thing you will need to win scholarships.

What is "The $cholarship State of Mind"?

Have you ever listened to the song "Empire State of Mind" by Jay-Z? If you have, you know it illustrates how New York (the "Empire State") is a breeding ground for successful, goal-oriented people. The song talks about many successful people who have come out of New York and chronicles some of Jay-Z's own success as a rapper.

The "$cholarship State" is like the Empire State in Jay-Z's highly acclaimed song. It is the condition in which your mind is completely prepared and ready to make you a scholarship winner. It is related to how you view yourself and a belief that you have the potential to win. A student who is in The $cholarship State of Mind picks up a scholarship application and says, "I have the potential to win this scholarship." A student out of The $cholarship State of Mind says, "I may have the ability to win this scholarship." The student in The $cholarship State of Mind puts their scholarship application in the mailbox and says, "I am going to win that scholarship." The student out of it says, "We will see what happens." A student in The $cholarship State of Mind learns about a $5,000 scholarship with an application deadline that is tomorrow, and the first thing they say is, "I was going to go to the game, but instead I am going to finish this application tonight and send it off tomorrow." The first thing the person out of The $cholarship State of Mind says is, "I wish I had a few more days to finish; I already have something to do tonight." The student in The Scholarship State of Mind is asked to submit a résumé and personal statement for a $1,000 scholarship before the end of the day, and they submit it within an hour. The student out of The $cholarship State of Mind has not created these documents beforehand, so they miss the opportunity. The student in The $cholarship State of Mind student says, "It is my responsibility to finish on time." The other student says, "My recommendation was late, so I could not turn the application in on time."

Do you see the differences between the student in The $cholarship State of Mind and the student outside of it? One is optimistic, the other pessimistic. One is certain, the other doubtful. One fully believes in their ability to win, the other is unsure of their ability to win. One is always ready to win; the other is only ready to win sometimes. A person in the Scholarship State of Mind is:

- **Confident**—certain in their abilities

- **Optimistic**—has a positive attitude related to winning
- **Focused**—is willing to sacrifice to win
- **Prepared**—has put in the time and effort to win at any moment
- **Responsible**—is accountable for both winning and losing

These are the out-of–the-ordinary qualities you have to develop if you want to be in The $cholarship State of Mind, and they are the same qualities you will need in order to be a winner.

Why is "The $cholarship State of Mind" Important?

The $cholarship State of Mind is important because without it, you will not be mentally prepared to win. Nothing reminds you of how important mental preparedness is better than failure. A time when state of mind contributed to my own failure was during my AP macroeconomics class junior year of high school. There was a big test that I just knew I was going to fail before the teacher even handed it to me. I felt this way because I did not take good class notes the week before, and I did not take much time to study. When the test was placed on my desk, I quickly glanced over it to see—

unsurprisingly—that I knew almost none of the material. Sure enough, when I got the test back two days later, it also came as no surprise that there was a large red *F* at the top.

In this situation, it is fair to say that I was not in The $cholarship State of Mind. I was irresponsible, pessimistic, doubtful, and most of all, unprepared. The outcome of the situation was that I received a failing grade. Now this was just a simple example of how not being in The $cholarship State of Mind could be detrimental to your success.

However, when scholarship money is on the line, the stakes are much higher. This was the case during the May of my junior year in high school, when my school's financial aid advisor informed me of a $1,000 grant opportunity. She told me she needed a personal statement and résumé by the end of the school day. This was during my lunchtime; I had class in twenty minutes and did not have access to computer at home. If I was unable to come up with a personal statement and résumé in twenty minutes, I would have lost the opportunity. Fortunately, I already had a résumé and personal statement on my flash drive, and they only needed a quick five-minute edit before I submitted them. The advisor was shocked because the documents were extremely detailed, yet I turned them in so swiftly.

About a month later, I received the grant and was able to purchase my first personal computer. Having ready access to a computer and the Internet was life-changing for me, as it allowed me to do many great things my senior year of high schools that would have been physically impossible without the generous grant I received. Some would call it luck or serendipity, but I would call it being in The $cholarship State of Mind. I was **focused** enough to stay inside and complete the documents instead of going outside for lunch, I was **responsible** enough to have brought my flash drive with me to school, I was **confident** enough to trust my abilities to win, and most of all, I was **prepared** enough to have the documents already created. This is why being in The $cholarship State of Mind is so important if you want to win scholarships. It will be the factor that determines whether you receive an *F* on your next AP macroeconomics test or a $1,000 grant to buy your first personal computer. The saying "your attitude, determines your latitude" perfectly sums up the role state of mind will play in your race for scholarships. If you only remember one thing about The Scholarship Race, remember that the way in which you approach the race for scholarships will determine the final size of your scholarship piggy bank.

The last and most tangible example I have to illustrate how The $cholarship State of Mind is important is the amalgamation of scholarship winners I have had the pleasure of meeting and becoming friends with during my scholarship journey. These wonderful and inspiring friends—who hail from California to Sri Lanka, Puerto Rico to Chicago, Chattanooga to New Jersey, and Utah to New Mexico—all have it. They each possess The Scholarship State of Mind. They have laser-like focus, they have made great sacrifices to be winners, they are confident in their abilities and potential, they do not run away from responsibilities, they prepare themselves to be winners, and they remain optimistic even in the face of adversity. These friends have started non-profit organizations, volunteered countless hours, been at the top of their class, and have made the decision to be winners in various areas of their lives. Though you probably have not met these great friends of mine, they serve as my real world examples that The $cholarship State of Mind is universal and tangible. The students who consistently win scholarships possess The $cholarship State of Mind, and those who consistently lose simply do not. The only question that remains is, do you want to be a consistent winner or a consistent loser?

How do I develop "The $cholarship State of Mind"?

Applying the $cholarship State of Mind to your daily life will be one of the most difficult steps you take while competing in the race for scholarships. However, like most difficult steps in life, it is a step down a path toward success. To help you with this, I will take a cue from one of my favorite books: Hill Harper's *Letters to a Young Brother*. It is filled with profound thoughts on how to turn ideas into reality. One of the main pieces of advice I took away from the book was the power of using mantras to achieve short-term and long-term goals. A mantra is a saying or phrase that you repeat during a meditation to calm your mind and to focus your energy. An example is, "Today is going to be a great day." If you repeat this phrase in the morning every day before you go to school, you will calm your mind and focus your energy on the school day being a good one, both unconsciously and consciously affecting the outcome of your day. Mantras are powerful tools to help you focus your energy, and they can assist you in finding and staying in The $cholarship State of Mind. The mantras you will read shortly are the exact mantras that helped me get into The $cholarship State of Mind in high school and in college, and I am confident they can help you negotiate various situations you may face inside and outside of school.

The $cholarship State of Mind™ Mantras

Situation # 1: You are in class, and you feel that what you are currently doing does not have anything to do with your future success.

Mantra: "I have to do this work now if I want to be a winner later."

Situation # 2: You are working on scholarship applications and you get discouraged because they are difficult.

Mantra: "I am a winner, and winners do not quit."

Situation # 3: You are about to send a scholarship application by mail or submit on an online scholarship application.

Mantra: "I am a winner, I am going to win this scholarship."

Situation #4: Your friends are calling you to come to a party on a Friday, the same day your scholarship application is due. You want to go to the party to relax, but you haven't finished the application yet.

Mantra: "I am a winner, and winners make sacrifices."

Situation # 5: You are about to go into an interview for a scholarship and you are feeling nervous or jittery.

Mantra: "I will come out a winner"

For All Other Situations

Mantra: "I AM A WINNER."

Did you notice that the word *winner* is in every mantra? This is because you have to constantly believe you are a winner if you want to constantly win. By taking the time to read this book, you have made the decision to sacrifice your precious time to learn about how you can succeed in the race for scholarships; this shows me you are ready to be a winner. Continue to remind yourself that you are a winner by saying the given mantra out loud three times in a row anytime you encounter a situation where you need or want encouragement. If you want to take it a step further, close your eyes and breathe slowly, then repeat the mantra three times out loud. By repeating these mantras, you force doubt out of your mind, you encourage yourself to keep going, and you focus your energy on winning. This is the only way you will remain in The $cholarship State of Mind—by constantly reminding yourself that you are a winner, even when the odds are stacked against you, even when your classes become difficult, even when you are stressed out over the scholarship application process, and even when you have to sacrifice. Once you are in The $cholarship State of Mind, winning will become less difficult because you wholeheartedly understand and embrace that winners work hard, winners are optimistic, winners do not quit, winners make sacrifices, and most of all, winners overcome failure.

PRACTICE MAKES...
BETTER:
WINNING
WHILE PEOPLE
AREN'T
LOOKING

Practice Makes ... Better

Three years ago, after listening to me talk about what I wanted to achieve in life, my mentor asked me, "So what are you doing today, so that you can achieve those future goals tomorrow?" I did not have a response for him, and that was truly a *eureka* moment for me. I realized that day that dreams and goals are like potential and kinetic energy. We all have potential energy (dreams), but potential energy cannot do any work. We have to learn how to turn dreams into goals so that our own potential energy can be turned into kinetic energy, which can do work. It is only through our actions that we see dreams become a reality.

I also learned that day that we are all born with the ability to capture our dreams, but very few people ever turn their dreams into a reality. I believe this is because few people know how to turn their dreams into goals. You see this in your everyday life—people who feel that just because they have dreams (to become an astronaut, to travel the world, to be wealthy) that these dreams must come true. These people feel that they are entitled to their dreams without having to work for them. What these individuals do not realize is that without action, dreams will remain dreams.

Four years ago, I dreamed of going to college for free, knowing almost nothing about what I would need to do in order to realize that dream. In addition to not having the necessary information to achieve this dream, I did not have the necessary work ethic. My grades were mediocre, I was extremely lazy, and my attitude could stink up an entire room. Basically, I was not turning my potential energy into kinetic energy. If I had not made the decision to turn that dream into a goal by learning about undergraduate educational requirements, tailoring my class schedule to be more rigorous, doing well in my classes, and most of all, asking for help from others, my dream would still be just a dream.

For many people, making the decision to turn their dreams into goals is a time-consuming one, but it does not have to be for you. Before you finish reading this paragraph, I want you to make the decision to turn your collegiate and financial aid dreams into goals. I want you to decide right now that from this point forward; you will work as hard as you possibly can to get the best grades, to search and apply for scholarships, and to win money for your education. Take control of your dreams; do not just sit and wish that they come true. Trust me: great things will start to happen because of it.

I was a varsity swimmer for three years in high school, and my coach, Mr. Roberts, would constantly drill the team on the basic things that would help us win races. *Practice, practice, practice* was Coach's philosophy. Practice in the morning, practice after school, and practice on the weekends. We practiced until the chlorine in the pool ate away at our skin and our muscles burned. At the time, it was difficult to understand exactly why our coach was so adamant about practice. Today, I see the beauty in his mentality. My coach knew that without practice, no matter how much collective talent we had, we would never reach our potential as a team. He knew that practice was key to the team winning swim meets.

After three years of swimming under Coach Roberts, I had mastered the four components I would need to win scholarships:

- **Practice**
- **The Start**
- **The Sprint**
- **The Finish**

These are the four components that led us to two conference championships, and they are the components that will lead to you winning scholarships.

Coach would emphasize that the four race components built upon each other, with practice being the foundation. Because of this, I like to think of the scholarship race components as blocks that come together to form a pyramid. Let's call it the **MillionDollar$cholar Scholarship Race Pyramid**™. You may be thinking, what about The $cholarship State of Mind, isn't the most important component? Indeed it is! That is why it sits at the base of the pyramid.

MillionDollar$cholar Scholarship Race Pyramid™

The pyramid is a great structure with which to visualize the components of The Scholarship Race, because the pyramid shows that each component provides a foundation for the next component until you reach the peak of the pyramid. Notice that The $cholarship State of Mind is the widest component and takes up the greatest area of the pyramid. Also note that each consecutive component is less wide and takes up less area of the total pyramid. Remember that developing and keeping yourself in The $cholarship State of Mind will be the foundation of your success. Just like a house, if your foundation is unstable, anything that you place on top of it will be unstable and may eventually collapse. It is important that you keep a solid foundation by continuing to remain in The $cholarship State of Mind with any and everything you do related to scholarships so you can build a completed Scholarship Pyramid that is stable.

Practice is the first component built upon The $cholarship State of Mind. The one quote that most people know related to practice is that old saying *Practice makes perfect*. Sounds great, doesn't it? *Practice* and *perfect* both start with the letter *p*, and they both have two syllables. It is also makes sense logically. It seems genius!

But the genius part of that statement ends there. If you want to be a scholarship winner, I need you to toss this idea out of your mind. Now that your mind is clear, let me replace it with a different idea: *Practice makes better.* You see, no matter how much you practice, it will not make anything you do, perfect.

It is important that you remain realistic during the scholarship process, because sooner or later, you will face difficulties. I say this because I have spent countless hours putting together winning scholarship applications, but I have also put together losing scholarship applications. I have used the same scholarship essay on two different scholarship applications (which will be explained later), and won one of the scholarships while not winning the other. You will also experience times when you feel that all your hours of practice are not paying off, or you may experience a time when you are not announced as a winner. This is because The Scholarship Race is a perfect (pun intended) example of *practice makes better.* It will be difficult in the beginning, and may become frustrating at times. But if you continue to practice, you will constantly get better and more efficient at applying for and winning scholarships. After hours and hours of more practice, will you be perfect? No. But you will be in a much better position to win.

Practice in The Scholarship Race begins with researching and identifying scholarships you qualify for. Here's a simple rule to always remember: *The only scholarship that you are guaranteed to lose, is the one you do not apply for.* If you do not know about a scholarship opportunity, how can you apply for it? This question confuses and hurts many students, because they do not know where to start finding scholarships they qualify for.

Start developing your general list of scholarships by intensely researching the colleges and universities that you plan on applying to or already have applied to. Go to the financial aid pages on the Web sites of these institutions and identify any scholarships or grants that you meet the requirements for.

33

Scholarship databases such as Scholarships.com™, which allow you to create a specific profile and view thousands of scholarship opportunities, are great online resources. The next resource is your high school. It was amazing how many seniors in my class would walk right past huge posters with phrases such as, "five thousand dollars for college" boldly written across them. Our post-secondary counselor made a binder full of scholarship opportunities, yet hardly anyone at my school put it to use. I would take a notebook and write down the information on those posters, and I would go home and study all the information I retrieved from that binder. Take advantage of any opportunities that your high school or college has posted on billboards, walls, etc. These opportunities are often exclusively for students in the area (which will mean less competition) and most students do not pay any attention to them. Lastly, learning about scholarships via word of mouth will be extremely important in helping you discover opportunities not posted on websites, posters, or packets. Do not be afraid to ask teachers, administrators, or mentors about scholarship/ financial aid opportunities that they are aware of.

While you are using all of these resources to research and identify scholarships, create a scholarship table like the one shown in the **MillionDollar\$cholar Scholarship Table**™ (pg. 37). This will help you track the progress of each scholarship or grant you apply for. The scholarship table should list the following information:

- **Scholarship name**
- **Dollar amount of award**
- **The number of essays needed and if they have been completed**
- **The number of recommendations needed and if they have been completed**
- **Whether a résumé is needed and if it has been completed**
- **Whether a transcript is needed and if it has been sent**
- **Deadline date**

- **If you have submitted the application for each scholarship you have identified**

Since there are many components to each scholarship, the scholarship table will help you break down your application for each scholarship into smaller tasks. This will help you to spread out the time you spend on each application and make the process less strenuous. As soon as you find out about a new scholarship, add it to your scholarship table. Do not procrastinate, because there is no time to waste. By adding scholarships to the list as soon as you hear about them, the table will become a very effective tool, informing you of the status of each scholarship so that you can complete each scholarship application at least two weeks early, instead of the day before the deadline.

MillionDollar$cholar Scholarship Table™

NAME	$$$	# ESSAYS DONE?	# RECOM. DONE?	RÉSUMÉ DONE?	TRANS	DEADLINE COMPLETE
Dell	20,000 & Laptop	3 Yes	1 Yes	No	None	Feb 1 Yes
UNCF	10,000	2 Yes	2 Yes	No	Sent	Feb 1 Yes
PNC Bank	40,000 a year	7 No	3 Yes	Yes Yes	None	Jan 31
Ohio State	10,000	2 No	1 Yes	Yes Yes	Sent	Mar 1

Note! *The information in this table <u>may not be accurate.</u>*
This is only an example.

Once you create and begin to fill in your scholarship table, post it somewhere where you will easily see it and look at it at least once a day. Just like a mantra, the list is only good if you constantly use it to help you. By posting the scholarship list in a place that is in clear sight, it becomes harder to ignore the fact that you have scholarship applications to complete. Try your best to quickly review this list at least once a day. Once a week, you should thoroughly review the entire list to make sure that you are staying on track with getting essays done, obtaining recommendations, completing résumés, and finishing the applications.

An interesting thing about practice—whether you are practicing for academics, sports, or hobbies—is that the majority of people do not see you when you are practicing. In most cases, people only see the finished product: an *A* on your report card, a free throw you made in the big varsity game, or one of your paintings on display in the school's annual art exhibition. In each of these examples, other people will observe and judge something for mere seconds to minutes that took you hours upon hours to learn how to do or create. The people observing did not see the amount of practice you had to put in to achieve your feat.

This is exactly how The Scholarship Race will be: The people who observe you winning will not see the countless number of hours you spent practicing in order to win. You have to understand that winning does not happen the day of report card pickup, the day of the game, or the day of the exhibition. Winning happens in the library when you are studying, in the gym shooting free throws, and in the art classroom practicing the techniques needed to create a great sculpture. Winning happens on all of the days you are practicing. Winning is in the exhaustion, winning is in the sweat that drops on the gym floor, and winning is in the all the clay that didn't turn out so beautiful. So if you want to be a winner in the scholarship race, you have to be ready to get exhausted, you have to be ready to sweat, you have to be ready to get frustrated, and most of all, you have to be ready to work while people aren't looking.

THE TAKEOFF:

DEVELOPING A STRONG FOUNDATION

The Takeoff

In a swimming race, The Takeoff (or the start) determines who hits the water first and who will take an early lead. Having a great takeoff sets a swimmer up for winning the race; having a bad takeoff means that a swimmer will be playing catch-up for the rest of the race. The Scholarship Race also has a takeoff, and the winners do not play catch-up—they take an early lead and use this lead to dominate the rest of race. Looking back at The MillionDollar$cholar Scholarship Race Pyramid, notice that The $cholarship State of Mind and Practice make up about 60 percent of the pyramid. You are only three steps away from the $, but in order to get there you have to master The Takeoff so you can build the remaining 20 percent of the Scholarship Pyramid.

MillionDollar$cholar Scholarship Race Pyramid™

The Takeoff in the race for scholarships consists of you completing or submitting the actual scholarship application components, including the scholarship essay/personal statement, recommendations, résumés, and transcripts. This is why each of these components has a separate column in the **MillionDollar$cholar Scholarship Table**—they each need to be monitored separately because they are the most important parts of the application. Some scholarships may not require certain sections (such as a résumé or recommendation), but you should always have these components prepared beforehand just in case.

No matter which components will be required for a scholarship application, they each will play a role in helping you become a winner, so they will all require a great amount of attention and effort to create. If someone attempts to tell you that your résumé is more important than your personal statement or that your personal statement is more important than your recommendations, *do not listen to them*! Some scholarships have over 40,000 annual applicants competing for awards. If a scholarship has this many applicants and only one hundred winners, in the end there will be many more losers than winners. If you want to be competitive, every part of your application has to be considered important; from the big to the small. What would a scholarship judge or committee member think if you turned in an application that had a recommendation that made you seem like the best thing since the iPod, but you turned in a résumé that made you look like a portable CD player? They would question the person who wrote a recommendation that appeared to overstate your abilities. This judgment would make it much harder for you to win. Avoid these types of situations by assigning equal importance to each of your application components.

The writing samples—either scholarship essays or personal statements—are a critical portion of your application because they show how well you can articulate your personal experiences, past accomplishments, and future aspirations. While reading your essays, the reviewers should catch a glimpse of your personality and your passions. Your writing should show that you have potential to write at the college level. If your essay reads like an elementary student wrote it, your chances of winning will decrease dramatically. You want to find a way to be creative and eloquent while still conveying a central message or thesis like you would in a paper for your English class. Creativity and eloquence will keep the reader interested in your writing, but your message or thesis will have them nodding their head in the end because they actually learned something after reading it.

The best way to keep the reader interested while still conveying a message is to *tell the reader a story*; don't write like you would for a research paper. Once you draw the reader in with a story, expand on the story with your body paragraphs. After the body paragraphs, wrap your writing up with a strong conclusion that shows what you learned from the story and how that story made you a better person. Every time you complete any writing sample for a scholarship application, send it to your e-mail (so you can always download it in case of electronic malfunctions) and save it to your computer and a flash drive so you can easily revise it and possibly use it for subsequent applications. Scholarship essays and personal statements for scholarships do not all have the same objective, though. Let's explore the objective of writing a **scholarship essay** and what makes it unique.

The Scholarship Essay

The scholarship essay is different from a personal statement in that *it is a response to a prompt or question the organization awarding the scholarship or grant gives or asks you.* You cannot choose the topic like you would in a personal statement. Here's an example of a **prompt** for a scholarship essay:

> *"We believe that gaining a college education is not only a great experience, but it is also a great responsibility. Tell us how gaining a college education would bring responsibility into your own life."*

And here's an example of a **question** that may be asked for a scholarship essay:

> *"If you were given $100,000 tomorrow to help contribute to solving any issue in your community, what would it be, and why?"*

The first thing you should ask when writing a scholarship essay is: Did I answer the prompt or question completely? This is a step that many students fail to take as they spend hours writing a great essay that only slightly attempts to answer the prompt or question given. To bring it all together, a great scholarship essay answers the given question or prompt in detail with a creative spin. To help you understand what a winning scholarship looks like, I have provided the essay I used to win a scholarship that focused on giving back to the community.

Winning Scholarship Essay Example

QUESTION: *If you won one million dollars tomorrow, what would you do with it, and why? (300 words or less)*

I have been in the foster care system for fourteen years of my life, and through it, I have observed the detrimental affects that this system has on students' performance in school. I believe that K–8 students who have been in or are currently in the foster care system are some of the most fragile; without help, they are likely fall victim to the horrible psychological and socioeconomic affects of being a foster child. Unfortunately, my community does not have many resources geared towards helping these students do well in school and cope with their personal struggles. Throughout my life, I have had people want to help and invest in my vision; people such as mentors who have cultivated qualities that have no physical measure. Their investments serve as my inspiration to come back to my community and help adolescents who are like me, and if I won one million dollars tomorrow, I would allocate a great portion towards the opening of a not-for-profit community organization and community center that provides free tutoring services, after-school activities, counseling, scholarships for high school seniors, technology grants for underprivileged children, and mentorship service. The organization's mission would be to provide services for adolescents who are underprivileged, lacking family support, and in need of inspiration, just as I was in need. My participation in the organization would provide me with great pleasure because I

48

could make an impact in the lives of children that do not have mentors or family members with the resources conducive to helping them develop into future leaders within their communities. I am positive that this organization would be a catalyst to assisting disadvantaged children in synthesizing their own success stories, children who would otherwise be overlooked by their community.

This sample directly answers the question given. In the response I included the words *if I won one million dollars tomorrow, I would ...* This statement directly answers the question by including those trigger words. Did you also notice that I included these words in the middle of the response instead of at the beginning? This contributed to the creativity of the essay, because opening with the trigger words *if I won one million dollars tomorrow, I would ...* is how the majority of students applying for this scholarship would respond. Instead, I opened by telling the reader something very personal about myself. This was meant to draw the reader in and open their mind and heart to my subsequent words. I then went on to

49

directly answering the question. Utilizing a creative approach will make the reader better able to absorb the message of your words. So remember for any scholarship essay: Be creative and always answer the question thoroughly.

The Personal Statement

The phrase *personal statement* is somewhat self-explanatory. It's a piece of writing that makes a *statement* about who you are as a *person*. It does something that a grade point average, test score, or award cannot: It gives you the opportunity to creatively tell the scholarship or admissions review board (the people who will read and judge your application) how high school has affected you. It also provides an opportunity for the review board to understand who you are outside of school. The review board will be looking for students who are well-rounded and understand that school is more than just acquiring accolades and gaining a high GPA or test score. School is about holistic (intellectual, spiritual, psychological, and emotional) growth and progression, and the people who read scholarship applications enjoy applicants who show that they understand this concept. The personal statement is your chance to show the review board that you understand this concept of growth and development, and in many instances it will be used to evaluate everything else included in your application.

Now that you see why the personal statement is so important, it's time to start writing. *Wait*! Before you start writing, review these Top Five Don'ts When Writing a Personal Statement. They are in reverse order to stress the most important don'ts.

MillionDollar$cholar's Personal Statement Don'ts

5. Don't use your entire personal statement to talk about your activities, honors, awards, and GPA, because they are already listed in the rest of your application. It is a waste of an opportunity to create a story that says something about who you are that the rest of your scholarship application cannot.

4. Don't start on the personal statement less than one week before the application is due. You will not have time to do the necessary revisions that will ensure you have a polished personal statement.

3. Don't make your personal statement longer than two pages if you are not given a word or page limit. More does not necessarily mean better. If you are given a word or page limit, follow directions! The scholarship judges will question your ability to pay attention and listen to more serious directions if you cannot follow simple word or page limits.

2. Don't tell a sob story simply because you believe this will make the review board feel sorry for you. Everyone experiences adversity, and the review boards hear hundreds (if not thousands) of sad stories. Instead of just focusing on the unfortunate things that have occurred in your life, focus more on how you overcame any adversities you have faced.

1. Don't submit a personal statement with multiple grammar and punctuation mistakes. The more errors you have, the more you appear unprepared for college-level writing, which will make it much harder for your personal statement to receive positive reviews.

Now that you know what you should not do when writing a personal statement, we can talk about what you should do when writing a personal statement. For this, I turn to two of my favorite hobbies—cooking and eating.

Writing a winning personal statement is like putting on a chef's hat and creating a great three-course meal. Though you may have never cooked a three-course meal, you may have enjoyed one at a restaurant or a gathering. Or maybe you've watched *Iron Chef* and observed the master chefs create a five or six-course meal. Even if you haven't done any of these things, it's okay. All you need to know is that a three-course meal usually consists of the appetizer, entrée, and dessert. These three very different components come together to form a very special, well-rounded, exciting, and fulfilling meal. The key thing to understand is that the courses *complement* each other. Each serves a different function, however, the meal would not be complete if any one of the courses was missing, and this is synonymous with your personal statements and scholarships essays. If they are missing any of the components, they will not be complete, and your chances of gaining acceptance into a school or winning money for your education will be lower. So how can you use the three-course meal analogy when writing? I will start by explaining the appetizer.

The *appetizer* is named so because it is supposed to stimulate your appetite. When a chef prepares an appetizer, s/he is creating a dish that will get you ready to enjoy the main course. The chef does this because if the appetizer is not that appetizing, guess what? Chances are the diner will not enjoy the main course as much. So the chef must ensure that the introduction to the meal is a hit. The appetizer is the equivalent to your personal statement's introduction. It has to be good, or the reader (AKA "the diner") will not want to keep consuming what you have written. A good introduction, like a good appetizer, stimulates the reader in a way that lets them know that the rest of the essay will be just as great—if not greater—than what they just finished reading.

The first thing you need to know to create a great appetizer is that appetizers must always appeal to the eyes, and sometimes the ears. The better food looks, smells, and sounds before you taste it, the better it usually tastes. This is because the brain gets your mind ready to enjoy good food through your senses. So you have to make the introduction appeal to eyes by making it look good and to the ears by making it sound good.

The second thing to know is that the appetizer is never heavy on the stomach. The appetizer is purposely kept small because chefs only want to stimulate your appetite with it; they do not want to weigh you down with so much food that you do not want to eat the entrée and desert.

Lastly, the appetizer is usually the time to get creative. Due to the small size of the appetizer and its goal of appealing to the senses, it is usually where chefs turn their crazy ideas into something that works. Well, your introduction should be a place where you turn the crazy ideas you have into something that works.

The next dish that comes out in a three-course meal is the entrée—"the main course." The title speaks for itself; however, to create a great personal statement, you need to know why it is called a main course. Two qualities make the entrée the main course: It is usually the most filling dish, and it usually is the most savory. Chefs put a great amount of time into the entrée because it is the center of the meal. A great appetizer and a great dessert do not mean much if you mess up the main course. The entrée is like the body of your personal statement.

What do you need to do to produce a good entrée? Well, you need to make sure that it is your main course. It has to be filled with content that expands on the introduction. Secondly, the content has to taste good. The content should be filled with different flavors that come together and create something that is savory and filling.

And then there is dessert—the sweet something at the end of the meal that leaves the diner satisfied and ready to shake the hand of the chef that prepared it. The dessert is fresh, it is small, and it is sweet. It is fresh in order to wake up the diner after a heavy main course, small so that the diner can enjoy it all, and sweet so that the diner completes the meal on a good note. Dessert equals your closing. It needs to be fresh, because the reader has already read a good amount of your writing; if you keep saying the same thing, you will bore the reader, and boredom will be the last thought they have about your personal statement. It needs to be small, because if your introduction and body were good, the reader is nearly full and does not want to eat too much more. Finally, it needs to be sweet, because this complements the savory appetizer and entrée and wraps up a great meal.

So now we have the recipe: one quarter appetizer (introduction), one half entrée (body), and one quarter dessert (closing). Once you start cooking, always keep in mind that there are many people who can compose a good essay, but only a select few can compose a winning essay. The key to creating a winning essay is understanding that every course in the meal is important, and that each course has its special qualities. The appetizer stimulates the appetite, the entrée is the main course, and the dessert is short and sweet.

That's enough time spent talking about cooking. Now it is time for you to get in the kitchen so you can sharpen your knives (pens and pencils), gather some produce, herbs, and spices (your ideas), and preheat your oven (your computer) so you can test the given recipe for a great personal statement.

Just remember that the personal statement is about illustrating who you are as a person in and—more importantly—outside of school. You want to find something that other parts of your application do not say, start early, be concise, be creative, and *revise, revise, revise!* Keep every hint in mind, maybe even watch an episode of *Iron Chef,* and you will be creating great personal statements in no time.

To illustrate how to properly use the three-course meal analogy, let's look at a personal statement I used to gain acceptance to several highly selective colleges and universities in the United States.

Winning Personal Statement Example

"Do Not Be Afraid of Drowning"

My head broke the surface of the water. I was sinking in a manner that restricted my lungs' ability to inhale air. "What was he thinking?" I asked myself as I descended into the depths of the water. As I took my second gulp of chlorinated water, "What was he thinking?" raced through my brain again. Surely I would drown in Kenwood Academy's 20 x 10 meter pool and be remembered as the ignoramus who could not swim but still jumped in the deep end of the pool on the first day of swim practice.

My instinct to survive kicked in as my adrenaline turned into a frantic dog paddle, propelling me to the poolside. My first breath above water was more refreshing than water on a hot day; never before had I been so happy to be able to breathe. I looked up to see Coach Roberts staring at me with a half grin.

"Are you okay?" he muttered, with a slight pause.

I responded, "What was that!"

"Well, you needed to get over your fears of the water," he told me in a tone that suggested what he did had perfect rationale.

If I had not been gasping for air, I probably would have stopped and thought that my coach was terribly right, but my mind was preoccupied with the chlorinated water playing in the bottom of my stomach. I stopped swimming for a couple of days after the incident, but my coach persuaded me to get back in the pool (the shallow end only, of course).

The weeks that followed were strenuous physically, but inspiration came when I could actually swim a lap by myself. Soon I could swim 100 meters without the help of the wall, then 200 and 500 soon followed. Never once did I stop to reflect on the exact moment I realized that the pool I could now gracefully dive into and swim 500 meters was the same pool I almost drowned in.

My epiphany came after I finished my first 500-meter freestyle (the longest event in competitive high school swimming) in an actual meet. I finished dead last in the event, but I finished. With the help of my teammates and coach—whose shouting during the entire event gave me the motivation I needed to keep going—I finished. When I got out of the water, just as exasperated as I had been when I almost drowned, my coach met me with another half grin. This made me think of his response the day I almost drowned. I finally realized why he made me jump into the deep end of the pool that day. It was not because he was crazy, and it was not because he took pleasure from watching me nearly drown. It was because he knew that my swimming the 500-meter freestyle in competition would be impossible without overcoming my fears; the only remedy was for me to just jump in the water.

Students are frequently taught that the value of a decision is based upon the amount of time spent evaluating that decision. But this moment helped me understand that sometimes we have to stop evaluating situations, allowing enough time for our fears to influence us, and we have to listen to our hearts. Running for Student Council President—even when I feared I was an unqualified and unprepared underclassmen—won me the position and priceless leadership experience, just as jumping in the pool when I feared I was going to drown, helped me develop into a better swimmer. Only in hindsight could I have realized that some of life's greatest moments come when we do not stop to think of our fears and we jump in; sometimes, we do not have to be "afraid of drowning" when it comes to life's pool of situations.

Do you think that my first sentence was fresh and colorful like an appetizer is supposed to be? Well, that was my goal. I wanted to make the first sentence fresh and colorful so that it would be both appealing to the eyes and the tongue so the reader would want more. I then followed up the appetizer with the main course, which in this case was the explanation of behind the opening story. In the main course, I wanted to expand on the introduction to ensure that the reader understood exactly what my personal statement was about. I also started to set up my closing paragraph (dessert), which would contain the overall message about what I learned about myself and about the world from the story presented in the appetizer. I made the dessert short and sweet; ensuring that I did not weigh the reader down, while still including the overall message I wanted to convey.

Scholarship Recommendations

The recommendation(s) give the reviewers an opportunity to see respected individuals' opinions of you, and they should accentuate the activities and information listed in the rest of application. They are so important because they represent the only part of the application not completed by you, and sometimes the quality of your recommendation (length, content, position of person who completes it) says much more about who you are as a person than anything you could say about yourself. This is why it is imperative that your recommendations be completed by someone that has had a close relationship with you (other than family members), someone who has observed your participation in different extra-curricular activities, and someone who is familiar with the scholarship you are applying to. Always give your recommenders at least three weeks to complete your recommendation, whether they are hard copies or online. When requesting a recommendation, simply ask the person writing the recommendation, "Would you like a copy of my personal statement and résumé?" Some will say they do not need these things, but most people will say that they would like copies. This of course means, you should have your personal statement or scholarship essay and résumé (résumés will be explained in the next section) completed before you request the recommendation. Whether the recommendation is submitted as a paper copy or online, always ask your recommender to save it so you can request it from them for future scholarships. Lastly, remember to follow these rules for requesting recommendations.

MillionDollar$cholar's Recommendation Rules™

1. All your recommendation(s) should be completed by people who have had a close relationship with you.

2. Your recommendation(s) should not be completed by a family member, even if your family member is one of your teachers, community leaders, or coaches.

3. Always give your recommender at least three weeks' notice to complete your recommendation.

4. Be prepared to give your recommender a résumé and personal statement so they can know more about your past activities and why you are qualified.

5. Tell your recommender to save your recommendations or make copies so you can easily use them later.

The Scholarship Résumé

A résumé is usually a one to two-page document primarily used to illustrate to a potential employer why you are qualified for a job. The résumé is basically you trying to sell yourself to someone in one to two pages of information. In the specific case of scholarships, the résumé is used to sell you to a scholarship committee or scholarship reader. The scholarship résumé is used to clearly show why you are qualified to win a scholarship by listing and persuasively explaining the following information:

- **Past work experience**

- **Past extra-curricular activities**

- **Summer or outside academic programs**

- **Past volunteer experiences**

- **Past leadership experience**

- **Any special awards or recognition you have received**

In many cases, the résumé you will be asked to provide as a part of your scholarship application will be called an *activity résumé*, because unlike an employment résumé, it really only highlights the activities you have participated in throughout your high school career. This does not mean you should compile an extremely detailed, bullet-point list of EVERY activity you have participated in during high school. Rather, you should only list the activities that have been the most relevant to you and that you have spent the most time participating in. You should do this because listing a bunch of activities that you have participated in without explaining them does not tell me much of anything about your work ethic or how meaningful the activities have been in your life. It only tells me that you have participated in a lot of extra-curricular activities. This is not the message you want to convey with your activity résumé. By only choosing the most meaningful activities you have participated in, you give yourself room to actually explain how you have participated in them and the impact they have had. This will leave a much more positive impression on the people whose job is to analyze your activity résumé.

Let me give you an example. I was helping a young lady at my alma mater in Chicago with a scholarship application. I asked her if she had an activity résumé, and she enthusiastically replied, "Yes!" I took a quick look at the résumé, and it looked something like this:

Unrevised Activity Résumé

MillionDollarScholar
Address:
E-mail:
Phone:

- Student Council Representative, Two Years
- Muntu Dance Ensemble Member, Four Years
- Volleyball Team, Two Years
- DePaul Summer Pre-Medical Program, One Year
- National Honor Society, Two Years

What does this activity résumé tell you about this scholarship applicant besides the names of the activities she has participated in and the numbers of years she has participated in them? This activity résumé leaves it up to the reader to answer what she did while she participated in the various programs and how they were meaningful to their high

67

school experience. This is a sure way to get your application thrown in the "looks great, but unfortunately ..." pile. Do not leave it up to the reader to do the difficult work; you want to clearly show them why you are a great student and why you deserve the scholarship. In your activity résumé, clearly tell the reader how a certain activity impacted you, how you impacted it, and how many years you contributed to the activity.

A revised version of the activity résumé listed above would look something like this:

Revised Activity Résumé

MillonDollarScholar
Address:
Phone:
E-mail:

- **<u>Kenwood Academy Student Council President</u>** (Two Years): As president, my responsibilities have been to organize school events and communicate with the administration. My experience as president has helped refine my definition of what it means to be an effective leader.

- **Muntu Dance Ensemble** (Four Years): Learned West-African Muntu choreography and various percussion techniques. We performed the choreography and percussion we learned in a culminating ceremony at the end of the program.
- **Kenwood Academy Volleyball Team** (Two Years): As co-captain of our women's varsity volleyball team, I helped lead our team to the State playoffs for the first time in school history.
- **DePaul University Summer Pre-Medical Program** (One Year): This two-week program exposed me to different aspects of preparing early to get into medical school. I visited local hospitals, met numerous medical students and researchers, and observed a human cadaver.
- **National Honor Society** (Two Years): Inducted into the Kenwood Academy National Honor Society Chapter in 2008. This is an honor that distinguishes students with a GPA greater than 3.5 who are leaders, athletes, and scholars.

This résumé looks more like a winners. It is much more detailed in that it tells me something about each activity and the impact it has had on you. The young lady did not have much time to revise her résumé, so we could only make quick changes to it. A final activity résumé should be even more sophisticated. The final version should be divided up into different activity categories (this helps the reader follow the information better) and specific activity dates. Each activity category should also have at least two activities listed and explained in each section. To help you better visualize this, I am going to show you a shortened version of the activity résumé I used in high school for every scholarship that asked me to provide one.

Winning Activity Résumé Example

Derrius L. Quarles
Address
Phone
E-mail

WORK EXPERIENCE

Biochemistry Research Intern: Rush University Medical Center (One Year)

Paid eight-week internship within Rush University Medical Center's Biochemistry department. I worked eight hours a day in a laboratory on assigned research topics.

Custodian and Apprentice: Final Kutz Barbershop (Three Years)

Ensured all windows, fixtures, bathrooms, and supplies within the shop were clean and sanitary for barber and customer use. Also trained in the basic techniques of barbering.

SCIENCE ACTIVITIES

Health Professions Research and Exposure Program (HPREP): University of Chicago Medical School (One Year)

I learned the requirements of getting into medical school and what to expect when I am in medical school. I visited local hospitals, met numerous medical students and researchers, and observed a human cadaver.

Med Day: University of Illinois in Chicago Medical School (Two Years)

Participated in full-day events in which I was exposed to medical lectures, presentations, and facts about the medical field. I learned how to take all the vital signs and observed several human cadavers.

EXTRACURRICULAR ACTIVITIES
Varsity Swimming Team: Kenwood Academy (Three Years)
This experience as an athlete taught me how to be a team player, and to be dedicated to all the goals I have in life. As a dedicated team, we succeeded in consecutively winning the South East sectional championship and having our team's two best seasons in the last ten years.
Nursing Unit Volunteer: La Rabida Children's Hospital (Two Years)
I volunteered four hours a week in the S.S. La Rabida ward. I spent time holding and playing with children, giving them attention. This is a great experience that is teaching me how to interact with children that have special needs and children of different ages.

LEDEARSHIP ACTIVITIES
Student Council President: Kenwood Academy (Two Years)
As president, my responsibilities have been to organize school events, communicate with the administrators about the wants and needs of the student body, and schedule student council meetings. My experience as president has helped me learn what qualities a great leader displays, and define what it means to be great leader.

Varsity Volleyball Team: Kenwood Academy (Two Years)

As co-captain of our boys' varsity volleyball team, I helped lead our team to the State playoffs for the first time in school history.

AWARDS & RECOGNITION

Chicago Bulls Sprite MVP: Chicago Bulls (Two Years)

Won an award honoring the top fifty African-American males in the Chicago Public School system. The honorees were chosen based on scholarship, extra-curricular involvement, and community service experience.

National Honor Society: Kenwood Academy (One Year)

This honor distinguishes students as leaders, athletes, and scholars. National Honor Society Members organize community service events and activities throughout the school year.

You should avoid common mistakes by observing these Résumé Don'ts:

MillionDollar$cholar's Résumé Don'ts

1. Don't allow errors in grammar, spelling, and usage to show up on your résumé.

2. Don't try to be to unique by making your résumé "pretty" by adding bright colors or photos of yourself.

3. Don't include false information on your résumé, up to and including your contact info and qualifications.

4. Don't submit a creased or stained paper résumé.

5. Don't make your activity résumé more than two pages. Even one page can be more than enough.

Finally, always remember that you want your résumé to make you seem like a star. It should not include any false or misrepresenting information, but it should make you seem like the best thing since the iPod. After you have created your activity résumé, you will have finished all four of the basic scholarship application components. Now all you have to do is bring these documents together so you can submit your application electronically or in the mail. For the scholarship applications that are completely online you will be required to enter the information in your activity résumé and other scholarship application components into various sections in the online application. This should not be very difficult if you have already created the scholarship application documents because you can simply copy and paste the information in your documents into your Internet browser.

Before you submit any scholarship application in the mail or online, you must always make some important last-minute checks. I call these steps The Finishing Touches. These steps take the a minimal amount of time, but they are still steps that, if ignored, can easily lead to your application being put in the "your great application was excellent, but unfortunately ..." pile. Do not allow all the hard work you have put into your application(s) to go to waste by not triple-checking each of these finishing touches on your scholarship application(s) before you click the "submit" button or put your application in the mail.

MillionDollar$cholar's Application Finishing Touches

1. The most important finishing touch is to ensure that you submit all of your applications at least two weeks before the deadline. Things can go wrong with the mail and the Internet, so beat the crowd and submit your application well in advance. Let me repeat this: SUBMIT TWO WEEKS IN ADVANCE! This means ten business days (Monday–Friday) in advance. If the application deadline is Jan 31st, submit or mail your application on or before Jan 15th. If the deadline is Feb 1st, submit your application by Jan 14th. This rule applies to any deadline date.

2. If you are submitting a paper application, ensure there are no stains on any of the papers you submit. Ketchup, mustard, and oil do not make a good impression. Even if you believe you wiped it off well, get a clean and stain-free sheet of paper.

3. If you are submitting a paper application, ensure that none of the pieces of paper have any creases or

unnecessary folds in them. If any do, replace them with a crisp sheet of paper.

4. After you have submitted an online or paper application, always confirm that your application has been received by calling or e-mailing the organization or contact person you sent the application to.

You now have all of the information you need to create a great scholarship application. What are you waiting for? Start working!

THE SPRINT: GETTING AHEAD OF THE PACK

Liquid water on the ground and in ponds, lakes, and rivers is converted into gas after being heated by the sun, forming clouds. When the atmospheric pressure changes, these clouds produce rain and snow, returning liquid and frozen water to the ground. Processes like this have occurred for millions of years, and humans could not survive on Earth without them.

They are also some of the most efficient processes known to man. Why are these natural processes so efficient? Because they recycle materials. These processes can occur over and over because the materials involved are simply reused with each new cycle instead of being created from some other source. Recycling is observed in many natural systems, and it is a very important concept for you to understand when competing in The Scholarship Race.

Up to this point, you got into The Scholarship State of Mind, practiced researching and identifying scholarships, and created your scholarship application components. You have developed the solid foundation needed to win by completing over seventy-five percent of The Scholarship Race Pyramid, but now you must learn how to get ahead of the pack of students you are competing against for scholarship dollars. To do this, take a lesson from the extremely efficient natural processes all around you and learn how to recycle.

You have written your personal statements and essays, received your recommendations, and created your résumé. Do you have the time to create those documents all over again? Of course not! If you tried, you would soon find it nearly impossible to complete all the scholarships on your list. The key to completing a large number of scholarship applications in a short amount of time is recycling. For example, instead of starting over on each scholarship essay, you can take paragraphs from the first few essays your wrote and insert them in the right places until you have an entirely new essay you can use for a different scholarship.

MillionDollar$cholar Scholarship Race Pyramid™

Recycling application components sounds like a fairly simple thing to do. The tricky part is that it can be an effective tool if used properly; however, if used incorrectly, it can be a quick way to lose a scholarship. In order to recycle effectively, you have to tailor each application component to the scholarship that you are applying for.

For example, if you are applying to a scholarship that awards money to applicants that have clearly shown academic achievement, it is not a good idea to use a recommendation previously written by a community service organizer, because that recommendation cannot speak first hand about your abilities in the classroom like a recommendation from a teacher can. Another example would be if you apply to a scholarship seeking successful student-athletes. For this application, you should not recycle an essay about your experiences volunteering in a hospital.

In order to tailor each application component you recycle, you must find out what each scholarship is specifically looking for in a winner. Visit the website for each scholarship you apply for, if it has one. If it does not have a website, ask a teacher or administrator at school if they are familiar with the scholarship and if they can give you any information that could help you win. If this fails, give the organization or entity awarding the scholarship a call and ask them general questions about the scholarship such as "Why was this scholarship originally created?" and "What overall qualities are you looking for in an applicant?".

In addition to the large changes you may need to make when you are recycling, you will also need to make small changes to your application components. For example, imagine you are applying for the Dell Scholarship, but the essay you are recycling states, "I feel I deserve the Wal-Mart Scholarship because ..." If you submit that scholarship essay with your Dell Scholarship application without changing the name mentioned, you just lost that scholarship. This is one example of how a small revision can make a big difference.

Consider that an application package is somewhat like a suit—it looks its best when it is tailored (tapered on the sides, pants and arms shortened to a certain length) to the person wearing it. Although it may look okay without tailoring,

83

it looks impeccable with it. The scholarship you are applying to is like the person wearing the suit. The scholarship application is the suit and you my friend, are the tailor. You are going to have make alterations in specific places if you want to tailor your recycled scholarship application components to the scholarship you are applying for.

To ensure that you recycle successfully every time, here are rules you should always follow when recycling application components to create a new scholarship application:

MillionDollar$cholar Recycling Rules

1. Ensure that each section of your scholarship application is tailored for the specific type of scholarship you are applying for. If it's a community service oriented scholarship, your recommendation(s) and essay(s) should focus on your experiences with community service. If it is a leadership-oriented scholarship, your recommendation(s) and essay(s) should focus on your leadership experiences.

2. You can recycle an entire essay or personal statement if it directly applies to the new scholarship. For example, imagine you wrote an essay in the past about your love for science. If the scholarship you are presently applying to is related to science and the essay prompt asks, "Why are interested in science?" you may be able to recycle that entire essay you wrote earlier and save valuable time.

3. Use different parts of past personal statements or essays to create entirely new essays. (Remember that a few paragraphs from old essays with a few new sentences added to them creates an entirely new essay.)

4. Ask your recommenders if you can have multiple copies of their recommendations. If they agree to give you multiple copies, make sure each recommendation copy has their signature on it or is in a signed envelope (if needed).

5. Always have extra copies of your résumé, standardized test scores (ACT, SAT), and FAFSA Student Aid Report (SAR). You will definitely need these items the majority of time when applying for scholarships. Having copies ready saves you valuable time.

6. Keep an electronic copy of all of your scholarship essays/ personal statements, and résumés on a flash drive. This will keep you prepared to take advantage of any opportunities that come your way without notice.

Following these rules will help you save time, reduce stress, and finish scholarship applications well before the deadline. REMEMBER: When used properly, recycling is not only good for the environment; it's good for your scholarship piggy bank as well.

A PHOTO FINISH: WINNING WITH STYLE

A Photo Finish

The process of juggling scholarship applications (even when recycling), school, extra-curricular activities, and other responsibilities can make the most organized person stressed. Over time, this stress can cause you to reach a point where you simply have no more energy left—a point called *burnout*. The problem with burnout is that it always happens right before the end of the race. You could be way out in front of the pack of other racers, and all of a sudden you start to slow down and the other racers are catching up to you or passing you by.

This can happen if you relieve stress by spending less and less time on your scholarship applications. Unfortunately, this is only a temporary fix. It will cut down on your stress in the short run, but it will also cause you to lose the race in the long run. At this point, you are only one step away from crossing the finish line. You have built a solid foundation that has put you ahead of the competition; now all you need to do is build the final ten percent of The Scholarship Pyramid. If you want to win consistently, you must learn how to balance all of your work so you do not sacrifice the time needed to complete your scholarship applications. By learning how to balance, you will be able to keep your grades up, participate in all of your activities, and still put in the time that is required to win The Scholarship Race.

MillionDollar$cholar Scholarship Race Pyramid™

91

Time I$ Money, Money I$ Time

Managing your time is the most effective way to help you balance and decrease stress. If you learn how to manage your time effectively, you will be able to fit more activities into your schedule because you will waste less time wondering what you are supposed to be doing or what you could be doing. In high school, I would sometimes come home, toss my book bag down, and go to sleep or watch television for a couple hours. When it was time to do homework, it was eight o' clock and I would ask myself where all the time went. This is a simple example of how not monitoring time will cause you to later ask where all the time went. Far too many students are familiar with this cycle of wasting time. In order to break this cycle, you must manage your time more effectively.

A combined planner/calendar will be the single most important time management tool you have. With a planner/calendar, you can plan and track your day by the hour. By doing this, you can see what you should be doing every hour; these reminders will help you keep track of what you have to do. When purchasing a planner/calendar, look for one that is small enough to carry around in your book bag. By carrying it around with you, your goal should be to use it at least once a day while in school.

Remember, a planner/calendar only works if you actually use it. If you purchase one but do not use it, you will waste your money and your time. Make sure that you fill it up with the work and activities in your schedule and stick to the goal of using it at least once a day while in school.

Once you begin to use your planner/calendar frequently, plan ahead as much as possible. Fill it with the things you know will have complete (such as scholarship deadline dates) as early as you can. Also, make sure you add items to your calendar as soon as you become aware of them, such as homework assignments, college fairs, events, and so forth.

Prioritize by completing your most important tasks first. This will ensure that you do not forget to complete a very important task by focusing on the small tasks first. For example, school is always going to be your most important task, so everything on your schedule should fit around school.

93

Scholarship applications should be at the top of your priority list after school. This means that you should undertake other activities only after you have completed tasks related to finishing school and scholarship applications. This does not mean you have to completely drop tasks that are not related to school and scholarship applications, but it does mean that you should fit these tasks in between things you have to do related to school and scholarship applications.

You should also spread your time out when completing important tasks. You do not want to try to complete an entire scholarship application in one day (unless you absolutely have to in order to meet a deadline), because it requires hours and hours worth of time. Spread out time-consuming tasks over different days and take breaks in between hours worth of work by doing relaxing things such as meditating, praying, deep breathing, listening to music, exercising, or doing nothing. By incorporating these relaxing tasks into your work schedule, you will avoid burnout and keep yourself fresh.

In addition to spending some time doing relaxing tasks in between many hours of work, you should take at least two days every two weeks to do only doing things that you enjoy. Put down your pencils, computer, homework, textbooks, and applications, and just spend the entire day doing things that make you laugh and enjoy yourself. I do not advise you to spend multiple days doing this because you would not get much work done; however, it is important for you to take these breaks. They will not only help you physically, socially, and emotionally, but they will also keep your mind fresh so that you can create great school projects, essays, and most of all, winning scholarship applications.

Wonders of the world such as The Pyramids of Giza and the Taj Mahal were not built in a day. They required great vision, skill, and dedication to create over a vast amount of time. Though scholarship applications are projects on a much smaller scale, you will not create them quickly either. Effectively managing your time will ensure that you do not have to cobble together an application that does not symbolize the quality of The Pyramids of Giza and the Taj Mahal. Use your planner/calendar, use relaxing activities, and use "me" days to help you keep your sanity while balancing

95

scholarship applications and life, and I am sure you will stay on track to win The Scholarship Race.

The Scholarship Interview

This is it. This is the culmination of all your hard work! Here's the only problem: For some students, the interviews will be it ... literally. Each scholarship you apply for will only choose a certain number of students as winners, and for the ones that include interviews; this number will usually be smaller than the number of students invited to interview. This is why the interview is so crucial; it may very well be the distinguishing factor between the student who outran the competition the majority of the race and tripped three steps before crossing the finish line and the student who remained focused until the very end of the race to gain a spot on the podium. If you want to be the student who slips three steps before the finish line, ignore preparing for the scholarship interview. But if you want to cross the finish line first, you have to set yourself apart, just as you did in your scholarship essay(s) and personal statement(s).

Speaking of personal statements, I like to think of the interview as another personal statement. But instead of providing a written statement regarding a personal experience, you make this statement in person. (Get it? Personal statement = statement you make in person.)

Just like a personal statement, a scholarship interview will have an introduction, body, and conclusion. In a subtle way, the interview will say something about your professionalism; your ability to express your thoughts, opinions, and experiences; your ability to remain cool under pressure; and how badly you want the scholarship you are interviewing for. You want to show a balance of all four of these key qualities: professionalism, eloquence, composure, and passion. I will break the interview down into an introduction, body, and conclusion that outline each of these four key interview components:

Scholarship Interview Introduction

Your appearance, posture, handshake, ability to maintain eye contact, the way you state your name, and overall attitude all add up to your introduction. When I say appearance, I mean that in every interview, your dress should be business casual and your grooming, makeup, jewelry, and so forth should make you look like you are ready to win. Lets cover some specifics.

MillionDollarScholar Interviewing Attire Guidelines

Ladies:

1. For every interview, wear a pant/skirted suit, or a suit-like pants or skirt, with a professional blouse.

2. You may wear a blazer over the professional blouse that does not match the skirt or pant color.

3. Your suit color should be navy, dark grey or a dark neutral shade.

4. If your suit or blazer is solid, try to wear a patterned blouse. If your suit or blazer is patterned, wear a solid blouse. These combinations complement each other.

5. Skirts should not sit above the knee.

6. Pantyhose should not have any runs and should be conservative in color.

7. Makeup should be minimal and accentuate natural skin tones. Do not apply extreme colors.

8. You hair should be styled professionally and you should not apply too much perfume.

Gentlemen:

1. Try your best to wear a suit to every interview.

2. If you do not have a suit, wear pressed khakis or slacks with a blazer or suit jacket over your dress shirt. If you do not have a blazer, just wear your dress shirt and slacks.

3. Your suit color should be navy or dark grey (charcoal).

4. Your dress shoes should be either black or dark brown. Make sure that your belt color matches your shoe color.

5. You can never go wrong with a solid white dress shirt.

6. No matter what color shirt you are wearing, if it is a solid shirt, wear a patterned tie. This can be polka dots, stripes, gingham, checks, boxes, paisley, plaid, etc. If your shirt is patterned, wear a solid tie. These are called *shirt and tie combinations*, and having a complementary combination screams *WINNER!*

7. Grooming is also a part of your attire, so make sure that your head and facial hair are neat and groomed.

8. Do not put on too much cologne.

Remember, an interviewer's first impression of you will not just come from your attire. It will also be determined by your greeting. If you have the opportunity to shake the hand(s) of the interviewer(s), place the web between your thumb and index finger in the web of the person's hand you are shaking. Your handshake should be firm but not overpowering; try not to shake hands for too long, five seconds is a good rule. Eye contact is a sign of respect and confidence, so always show respect by looking the person you are shaking hands with or talking to in the eye. You should be ready to say your first and last name confidently to each interviewer and tell the interviewer(s), "It is very nice to meet you." A positive greeting similar to this one will set the tone for the rest of the interview and help the interview transition away from the introduction. Interviewers will assess your professionalism throughout your interview, but the majority of

it will show during the introduction of the interview.

Scholarship Interview Body

The Scholarship Interview Body consists mostly of questions and answers. You should be prepared to answer any type of question. Questions usually fit into these various categories:

General—Questions every interviewee will be asked

Open-ended—Questions that cannot be answered with *yes* or *no* and need an explanation

Direct—Questions with one answer that do not necessarily require explanation

Spontaneous—Unique questions that not every interviewee will be asked

Interview Question Examples

General Questions:

- Why did you apply for this scholarship?
- Why do you deserve this scholarship?
- What makes you unique from the other applicants?

Direct Questions:

- What is your favorite subject?

- Do you have any siblings?

- Will you be a first-generation college student?

- What will your major be in college?

Open-ended Questions:

- Why do you enjoy leading others?

- How has being on the football team made you a better student?

- Can you tell me about a moment where you were treated unfairly?

- What do you see as your future career and why?

Spontaneous Questions:

- If you had one year to live, what would you do with that year?

- What do you want your legacy to be?

- If you could be any kind of fruit in the world, which one would it be?

- Is the cup half empty or half full?

You should prepare to answer questions from each category. Respond to each question truthfully and authentically. Do not try to answer the question the way you believe the person asking you the question wants you to. Be yourself! The easiest way to make an interview go bad is to be someone you are not. If you are not being yourself, it will show whether or not you think it will, so it is best to simply let your true self shine. Try to answer each question completely. Give a full answer, but do not talk unnecessarily. Finally, do not be afraid to throw some humor into your answers.

Every time you answer a question, you should answer it understanding that your words are not the only important part of your answer. Your tone and body language also play an equally important role. Your tone should be confident and excited, yet graceful and light. It should make the interviewers want to get to know you more and more. Your tone should be so swaying that when you leave the room after the interview time is up, the interviewers are somewhat disappointed because they wish they could talk to you longer.

When the interviewers are talking, give them your full attention and listen actively. Active listening includes shaking your head when the interviewer(s) say something that you agree with, making facial expressions, giving eye contact, and saying words or interjections that tell the interviewer you understand where they are coming from (such as "mmm hmmm," "right," and "ahhh"). Maintain a good listening posture by leaning slightly forward toward the interviewers. This shows them that you are interested in them and are absorbing their words.

Toward the end of the interview, the questions may get difficult. When you need time to gather your thoughts, it is much better to pause or repeat the question asked out loud to gather your thoughts instead of answering prematurely. By taking the time to gather your thoughts you avoid adding unnecessary sentence fillers such as "um," "ugh," and "like" between words that actually mean something.

You should come to the interview with some type of notepad so you can jot down a few quick notes if needed. To take these notes, you will of course need a writing utensil (preferably a nice pen). This ensures that you do not have to ask the interviewer for a pen if you have something to write something down.

Scholarship Interview Conclusion

This is the time to positively wrap up the impression you made during the introduction and body. This includes maintaining the same professionalism and great attitude you came in with, and reinforcing the answers you gave in the body. When the interviewers are almost done asking you questions, they will probably ask if you have any questions for them. Consider this the very last question of the interview. If you answer the question with, "No, I don't have any questions," you just failed the entire interview. Scholarship committees ask you this question because they want to see how interested you are in winning; they want to see if you have done your research and prepared. A great way to show them that you are not that interested or that you have not prepared is to not ask them any questions when given the opportunity.

When you get up to leave the interview room, make sure that you shake every person's hand in the room (if possible) and thank them for the opportunity. In addition to having a good interview introduction, body, and conclusion, follow these simple rules to ensure the best possible interview:

MillionDollarScholar General Interviewing Rules

1. Practice interviewing in the mirror two days and the day before your interview. Do not be afraid to literally ask yourself questions in the mirror and respond out loud to them. This will help you gather some potential talking points for the interview, reduce your anxiety or nervousness, and find your best interview voice. It may feel a little crazy asking yourself questions and responding to them, but you would much rather look crazy in a room by yourself than to look unprepared in a real scholarship interview. Trust me.

2. Develop one or two really good questions you would like to ask the interviewer(s) at the end of the interview.

These questions should clearly show that you have thought about the interview beforehand and that you are genuinely interested in the people interviewing you.

3. Your dress should always be business causal. While this is the time to put on the best clothes in your closet, just make sure that your attire makes a statement while still being subtle.

4. Always show up fifteen to twenty minutes early for an interview.

5. Turn your cellular phone on silent mode or off. This means it should not even vibrate during the interview.

6. Never check your phone during an interview. That message or call can wait!

7. Do not fidget your fingers or give attention to other items such as a pen while the interviewers are speaking.

8. Be confident in all your answers; you made it far enough to get the interview, so give responses that show the interviewers you deserve the scholarship.

9. Never leave the interview without showing appreciation to the interviewer(s) by saying "thank you" and that you look forward to communication in the future.

You worked hard to be chosen for an interview, and you deserve anything that you are awarded. Unfortunately, someone will have to "break it," so take this advice and come into the interview ready to be the applicant that "makes it."

Congrats! You did it. You worked hard enough to build the entire Scholarship Pyramid. Your muscles were aching, but you did not quit. You stayed in The Scholarship State of Mind. The sweat was coming down, but you kept practicing and took off like a rocket. You continued sprinting down the lane until you crossed the finish line a winner. A great philosopher once stated, "He who says he can, and he who says he cannot are usually both right". Well, I knew you could do it all along, and you knew you could too. The Scholarship Race was always yours to win and so are the many other races you will have to compete in during your life. Stay in The Scholarship State of Mind, and stay a winner.

The College Zone

Who Said You Can Only Win Money In High School?

Many undergraduate students end their first year of school with a significant amount of loans and out-of-pocket cost; forcing them to make the decision of either finding another school for the subsequent year or pausing their college education altogether. These are tough decisions for any student to make, especially after investing so much into education. I personally observed many friends go through these types of situation and I can tell you it is a very discouraging circumstance to face.

To avoid loans and out-of-pocket costs while in college, be aware of and apply for the enormous amount of scholarship money that is exclusively available to undergraduate students. Many students are unaware of the large amount of financial aid they could potentially earn while in college so they never look for it, and their debt keeps increasing. Do not put yourself in this situation. You can win

113

scholarships while in college based on a number of characteristics, including community service performed while in college, your family's income, the amount of loans you have accumulated for college, and your academic record while in college.

The first place you should start looking for scholarships is your college's financial aid office, where most schools post flyers or have a handout that lists scholarships available for students at the school. The next step is to go directly to your financial aid advisor and ask if s/he knows of any scholarship, grant, or employment opportunities available to you. If you are unsuccessful in finding any opportunities via flyers, handouts, or asking your financial aid advisor, schedule a meeting with your school's director of financial aid and ask them about ways of lowering your loan amounts and out-of-pocket costs. During this meeting, you must remember that many students come into that office every day in need of aid, so you must stress how important it is for you to receive additional aid if you are going to continue your education. The director may be able to tell you about grants and scholarships available to you directly from the school or external resources.

You should tap into your school's resources for financial aid first because most of the money your school has in its budget for financial aid becomes available at the beginning of the school year. The longer you wait to investigate, the smaller your chances become of receiving additional funds. The key thing to remember is **the earlier you inquire, the better.**

After you have tapped into all of your school's resources, you should then start searching for scholarship, grant, and employment opportunities outside of your school. A great place to start is an online scholarship database such as Scholarships.com. When using the database, narrow your search to scholarships and grants available to undergraduate students. After you have done this, you should find all of the scholarships you meet the requirements for, and you should make a MillionDollar$cholar Scholarship Table (pg. 136) to keep track of the work you need to do. Almost all of these opportunities will require a personal statement, recommendation, and/or résumé. I mention this as an FYI, since I know you are a pro at all of these things by now. If you need a quick refresher on these things, read through the Crash Course to Scholarships chapter at the end of this book. Because personal statements and recommendations become even more important in scholarship applications done in college, these components must be flawless. You must take your grammar, punctuation, and sentence structure to the next level, and your content should be more complex than anything you wrote in high school. This means that you should not recycle any writing you used in high school. Retire that writing, and only use it as inspiration to create fresh and even better writing.

Besides personal statements and recommendations, any scholarships you apply for as an undergraduate will rely more heavily upon your academic record. This means that doing well in your classes and having a strong GPA (3.0 or higher) will greatly increase your chances of being awarded most scholarships and grants. Your search for scholarships while in college may be a rough one, but it is definitely a search worth making if you need more funds to remain in school, decrease your debt, or cover some out-of-pocket expenses like books. If you utilize the information listed above in conjunction with the knowledge you have already gained from previous chapters, you too will soon be asking, "Who said scholarships are just for high school students?"

Funding Study Abroad Opportunities

If only money grew on trees. This feeling is common among college students, especially among those who desire to study abroad. This was exactly how I felt while planning a trip to study in Ghana over the summer after my freshman year in college. Every part of the trip had a cost associated with it. Visa: $100. Passport: $100. Immunizations: $175. The only thing that kept me sane during the entire process was the belief that traveling to another country to explore and experience the unknown was like a MasterCard: priceless. Instead of getting too discouraged, I stayed in The Scholarship State of Mind, and I won a $5,000 scholarship to help me fund the trip. Without that scholarship, I would not have had this academic experience.

During a study abroad session in Accra, Ghana, I realized how salient and life-changing traveling outside one's country truly is. It is an experience everyone should have at least once during his or her college career or life.

However, anyone who has ever done a study or volunteer abroad program during their undergraduate career will tell you how strenuous and tedious the entire process can be. It makes you constantly think, "If only money grew of trees!" Attaining your visa, getting the required immunizations and medication, and most of all, the program tuition and fees all cost money. No matter where in the world you travel, these fees quickly add up; on average, you will have to pay at least $2,000 to participate in a volunteer abroad program, $5,000 for a summer study abroad program, and $10,000 for a semester abroad program. I think I speak for most college students when I say that college is expensive enough as it is, and we cannot afford to casually spend thousands of dollars.

So, how can you get over the fact that money can't be found on tree limbs in order to go about funding such life-changing international experiences? First, you need to understand your funding options.

Just as there are a variety of undergraduate international programs, there are a variety of ways to fund such experiences. Depending on the description of the

119

program you are interested in doing (length and time of stay, location, if you are taking courses, if you are performing research), your financial aid options will vary greatly. In order to better help you visualize your funding options, I will compile scholarships and aid options into three lists: International Semester Programs, Summer Programs, and Volunteer Programs.

Semester Programs

- Governmental aid (Pell Grant)
- Institutional aid (merit or need-based scholarships and grants)
- Aid from academic departments
- Aid from the study abroad organization/company*
- Outside scholarships, grants, and fellowships*
- Fundraising*

Summer Programs

- Aid from academic departments
- Aid from the study abroad organization/company*
- Outside scholarships, grants, and fellowships*
- Fundraising*

Volunteer Programs

- Aid from the study abroad organization/company*

- Outside scholarships, grants, and fellowships*

- Fundraising*

Denotes aid that can be used for any program type.

Semester programs have the most funding options. This is the most ideal type of program because you will be taking classes abroad at the same time you would be taking them at your home institution, which allows almost all of the financial aid that you have received from the government and from your school to be transferred over to the school/program located abroad. If you have been accepted into this type of program, you should contact your school's financial aid office to start the process to transfer both your governmental aid and institution aid, including any Pell Grants and merit or need-based scholarships and grants.

Another uncomplicated way to earn funds is to meet with your academic department chair and director of international Affairs/ Study Abroad Programs to give them a description of the program you have been accepted to and to make a case as to why you should receive funding.

Summer programs have fewer options than semester programs, but they are also cheaper programs. You will usually not be able to use any governmental or institutional aid that has been designated for the academic year; however, this does not mean you cannot receive funds from your school. Like semester programs, you can schedule meetings with your academic department hair and director of international affairs and study abroad programs at your school in attempts to receive funds. You can also utilize the aid listed as *Aid that can be used for any program*.

Volunteer programs have the fewest financial aid options. Fortunately, they are also the cheapest type of international program. The only options that can be utilized for these types of programs are listed as *Aid That Can Be Used For Any Program*

Most international programs are handled by some type of company that specializes in sending students abroad and providing necessary international services such as insurance, transportation, and housing. These companies almost always have scholarship and grant opportunities, which you can find at there websites. These opportunities will be very scarce, so you must apply for them very early.

In addition to the financial aid opportunities from the specific study abroad company, you can use outside scholarships you have received to fund your program. For instance, if you received a scholarship from an organization in your hometown, you can ask the organization to allow you to use your funds for an international experience. Also, there are scholarships and fellowships specifically for students who want to study abroad, such as the Benjamin A. Gilman International Scholarship. Lastly, fundraising can be the difference between having just enough funds to complete your international program and staying at home. An important step in fundraising is drafting a letter that describes your program and why it is important for you to go. You can give this letter to family members, professors, churches, and community organizations. It should illustrate that you are passionate about going abroad, and it should move people enough to give you a small (or generous) donation. You can also raise funds using social networking sites.

Now that you are aware of your options, it's time to fund your international experience. Even if you will not be going abroad in the near future, it is best to plan early so that you can take advantage of all your options. Though money does not yet grow on the trees outside your dorm, you can still find the money you need to see the world.

I hope this has encouraged you to explore the world while you are in college. There are so many benefits to doing it. The costs may be high, but you will not regret it, especially if the majority of your funds come from scholarships. Dollars, Euros, and Yen, unfortunately, do not grow on trees, but you have something that is more valuable than money—The Scholarship State of Mind. If there is somewhere in the world that you want to see, I know that The Scholarship State of Mind can help you get there. Good luck and safe travels.

Your checking account is low. "I'll just call home," you say, but you soon learn that your parents refuse to send you any more money. "What about my savings?" Depleted, and you won't be receiving your work-study check for another two weeks. "Okay," you tell yourself, "I can make it through this." Then you open your mini-fridge to find it has become a vacant box, except for the ice cubes in the freezer. "I can make it though this" quickly transforms into "How am I going to make it through this?"

Unfortunately, this is a position many college students find themselves in at some point during the school year due to the many expenses that come with paying for college and surviving while there. There is no plan that can absolutely guarantee this will never happen to you; however, one concept, if put into practice, can help you make sure this hypothetical story does not become your reality. That concept is **money management**. Many college students do not

125

understand this concept well until they have a few freshman-year crises like the one above. This does not have to happen to you, though. You do not have to face an empty bank account and refrigerator to learn how to manage your money. Rather, by learning how to mange your money early, you can avoid the behaviors and habits that lead to such crises while in college. These are the three things all college students should understand when it comes to managing their money in college:

1. Frequent Purchases
2. Infrequent Purchases
3. Budgeting

Frequent purchases are ironic little things, in that they can easily make a huge impact on your funds without notice. Truth is, these small, frequent purchases— like gas, take-out, groceries, flying home, clothing, and entertainment—are what college students spend most of their money (not including financial aid) on. These small things trick many students because they do not seem like much at the time of purchase. It's easy to think that spending $40 on

126

clothes every day for a week is somehow less than spending $280 clothes in one day. And you can imagine that when you take all of your little purchases into account, the small things quickly add up to a large amount of money.

For example, if a student orders pizza two times a week at $20, that adds up to $200 a month. Then add on entertainment (movies, clubs, restaurants, bowling, etc.) at $30 a week, which adds another 150$ a month. If this were your budget, you would have just spent $350 on take-out and entertainment for the month! In order to alleviate spending large amounts of money on small things over time, you have to keep track of all your purchases, no matter how small they are.

Other ways of spending less on small purchases are to find discounts and by shopping smart. If you have a roommate, then you could buy food for the dorm with them and split the costs of dorm items such as TV's, mini-fridges, irons, ironing boards, and so forth. Utilize your meal plan as much as possible. Your school is going to get paid whether you choose one of their food options or not, so it is best to eat the free food served in the campus dining hall or eateries when possible rather than buying fast food or having food delivered. When buying clothing, find places that have quality clothing and good sales. There are also stores that will buy your used clothes and give you cash in hand for them. If you are buying things online, no matter what it is, always search for online coupon codes before purchasing, because it could save you 15–50 percent on your purchase.

The last frequent purchase where you could save a ton of money is airline tickets. Even if you only fly home two times a year, those tickets can still be ridiculously expensive.

Here are my suggestions for saving money on air travel:

- Buy your tickets as early as possible, because it will be cheaper
- Pack light, because baggage fees are steep
- Check out AirTran U, which offers students between the ages of 18–22 huge discounts on flights all across America.

Lastly, leverage the fact that you are a college student. Many stores and companies LOVE college students. From cars to clothes, companies offer all types of discounts and special offers. If you ever buy anything in a mall, ask if students receive discounts or if there is a program you can sign up for to receive discount coupons via e-mail or snail mail. If you buy things online, you can also find great coupon codes that can get you 5–50 percent off books, movies, electronics, and clothes.

Infrequent purchases usually cost a lot more up front, and for that reason we make them less frequently. For college students, these purchases usually include books, computers, printers, and summer storage for items too big to bring home. It's simple to save on these purchases: Research which stores or companies have the best price for what you need. When it comes to books, remember that your campus bookstore will almost always inflate the prices of textbooks 40 percent or more, and they offer you little money if you want to sell your books back. Even the used textbooks at your campus bookstore will be expensive when compared to online stores such as Amazon.com or Campusbooks.com.

When shopping for a computer, price should not always your primary concern. If a computer is cheap but will break in a year, then it is not your best option. Look for a computer in your budget that will last all of your college years. Also look for online discounts. Again, companies LOVE college students, especially computer companies. Always search for extra college discounts if you are purchasing online, or ask if you are purchasing in a store. The final trick that can lower your computer costs is to buy your computer and printer together as a package—even if your computer price isn't lower, you can get a free printer, which will come in handy.

Budgeting is the most important step to saving money in college. You should create a budget that allows you to live within your means while still saving a small amount of money every month. Create a spreadsheet that lists all of your income and expenses by category. Then set a cap for each expense so that you do not deplete your funds. Sign up for online access to your bank accounts to make it easier to stay aware of you spending. Also, avoid overdraft fees by not withdrawing more money than you have in your account, and by only going to ATM machines that do not charge you fees for withdrawals. Remember that the small things add up to a lot of money when you are in college, so monitor and limit your frequent purchases, find ways to save on infrequent purchases, and create a budget so that you always know where your money went and where it is going.

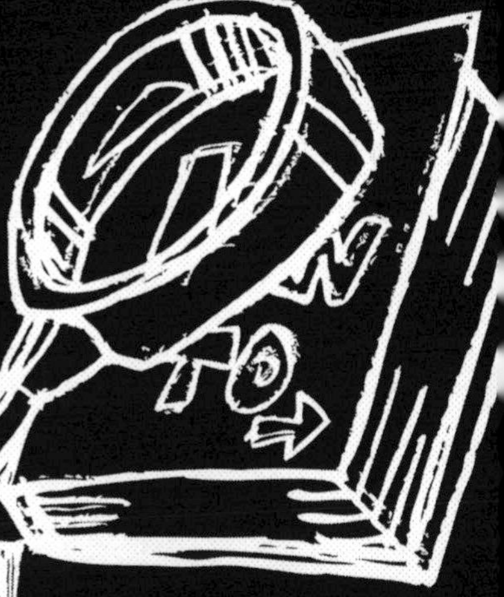

CRASH COURSE TO $CHOLARSHIPS

What if I condensed everything I've already said in this book so that you can refer to it when you start the scholarship process instead of reading the entire book over? Well, **MillionDollarScholar's Crash Course** is exactly that. The crash course will help you if you have a small question about a recommendation, if you forget what you need to do to create a great personal statement, or if you want to know what you should wear to the big interview. **This crash course will not replace everything that is in the rest of the book!** So if you are just starting out the scholarship process, I suggest you start reading from the very beginning of the book. But if you have already read the preceding pages and want a quick refresher of the information provided in any of the sections, the Crash Course is just for you.

The $cholarship State of Mind Mantras

Situation # 1: You are in class, and you feel that what you are currently doing does not have anything to do with your future success.

Mantra: "I have to do this work now if I want to be a winner later."

Situation # 2: You are working on scholarship applications, and you get discouraged because they are difficult.

Mantra: "I am a winner, and winners do not quit."

Situation # 3: You are about to send a scholarship application by mail or you are about to hit "submit" on an online scholarship application.

Mantra: "I am a winner. I am going to win this scholarship."

Situation #4: Your friends are calling you to come to a party on a Friday, the same day your scholarship application is due. You want to go to the party to relax, but you haven't finished the application yet.

Mantra: "I am a winner, and winners make sacrifices."

Situation # 5: You are about to go into an interview for a scholarship, and you are nervous or jittery.

Mantra: "I will come out a winner."

Situation # 6: You have just received an e-mail or letter telling you how great your application was, but unfortunately you have not been chosen as a scholarship recipient.

Mantra: "I am a winner, and winners grow stronger with losses."

For All Other Situations

Mantra: "I AM A WINNER."

MillionDollarScholar Scholarship Table™

NAME	$$$	# ESSAYS DONE?	# RECOM. DONE?	RÉSUMÉ DONE?	TRANS	DEADLINE COMPLETE
Dell	20,000 & Laptop	3 Yes	1 Yes	No	None	Feb 1 Yes
UNCF	10,000	2 Yes	2 Yes	No	Sent	Feb 1 Yes
PNC Bank	40,000 a year	7 No	3 Yes	Yes Yes	None	Jan 31
KFC	10,000	2 No	1 Yes	Yes Yes	Sent	Mar 1

Note! *Not all of the information in this table is accurate.*
These are only examples.

MillionDollar$cholar's Scholarship Essay Guidelines

1. **Make sure that you answer the prompt or question asked.** Take a second look at your essay to ensure that you answered every component of the question.

2. **Be creative.** Not only do you need to answer the question you need to do so in an interesting way.

3. **The scholarship essay is not a personal statement;** however, you should find a way to illustrate something about yourself in the essay.

4. *Revise, revise, revise!* The essay will say a lot about your writing skills, and if you make too many mistakes, the scholarship judges will question your ability to write at the college level.

MillionDollar$cholar's Personal Statement Don'ts

5. Don't use the entire personal statement to talk about your activities, honors, awards, and GPA, because they are already listed in the rest of your application. It is a waste of an opportunity to create a story that says something about who you are that the rest of your scholarship application cannot.

4. Don't start on the personal statement a week before the application is due. You will not have time to do the necessary revisions that will ensure you have a polished personal statement.

3. Don't make your personal statement longer than two pages if you are not given a word or page limit. More does not necessarily mean better. Follow the word or page limit listed in the application.

2. Don't tell a sob story simply because you believe this will make the review board feel sorry for you. Everyone experiences adversity, and the review boards hear hundreds (if not thousands) of sad stories. Instead of just focusing on the unfortunate things that have occurred in your life, focus more on how you overcame any adversities you have faced.

1. The more errors you have, the more you appear unprepared for college-level writing, which will make it much harder for your personal statement to receive positive reviews.

MillionDollarScholar's Personal Statement Do's

1. Tell a story that follows the three-course meal recipe: One-fourth appetizer (introduction), one-half entrée (body), and one-fourth dessert (closing).

2. Make a statement about yourself by telling an story interesting and creative.

3. Use any adversities you have faced as a platform to talk about your diligence and tenacity toward things such as academics, extra-curricular activities, volunteering, and so forth.

4. Ensure that your personal statement includes ideas that other parts of your application do not.

5. *Revise, revise, revise!*

MillionDollarScholar's Recommendation Rules™

1. All your recommendation(s) should be completed by people who have had a close relationship with you.

2. Your recommendation(s) should not be completed by a family member, even if your family member is one of your teachers, community leaders, or coaches.

3. Always give your recommender at least three weeks' notice to complete your recommendation.

4. Be prepared to give your recommender a résumé and personal statement so they can know more about your past activities and why you are qualified.

5. Tell your recommender to save your recommendations or make copies so you can easily use them later.

MillionDollar$cholar's Résumé Don'ts

1. Don't allow errors in grammar, spelling, and usage to show up on your résumé.

2. Don't try to be to unique by making your résumé "pretty" by adding bright colors or photos of yourself.

3. Don't include false information on your résumé, up to and including your contact info and qualifications.

4. Don't submit a creased or stained paper résumé.

5. Don't make your activity résumé more than two pages. Even one page can be more than enough.

MillionDollar$cholar Application Finishing Touches

1. The most important finishing touch is to ensure that you submit all of your applications at least two weeks before the deadline. Things can go wrong with the mail and the Internet, so beat the crowd and submit your application well in advance. Let me repeat this: SUBMIT TWO WEEKS IN ADVANCE! This means ten business days (Monday–Friday) in advance. If the application deadline is Jan 31st, submit or mail your application on or before Jan 15th. If the deadline is Feb 1st, submit your application by Jan 14th. This rule applies to any deadline date.

2. If you are submitting a paper application, ensure there are no stains on any of the papers you submit. Ketchup, mustard, and oil do not make a good impression. Even if you believe you wiped it off well, get a clean and stain-free sheet of paper.

3. If you are submitting a paper application, ensure that none of the pieces of paper have any creases or unnecessary folds in them. If any do, replace them with a crisp sheet of paper.

4. After you have submitted an online or paper application, always confirm that your application has been received by calling or e-mailing the organization or contact person you sent the application to.

MillionDollar$cholar's Recycling Rules™

1. Ensure that each section of your scholarship application is tailored for the specific type of scholarship you are applying for. If it's a community service oriented scholarship, your recommendation(s) and essay(s) should focus on your experiences with community service. If it is a leadership-oriented scholarship, your recommendation(s) and essay(s) should focus on your leadership experiences.

2. You can recycle an entire essay or personal statement if it directly applies to the new scholarship. For example, imagine you wrote an essay in the past about your love for science. If the scholarship you are presently applying to is related to science and the essay prompt asks, "Why are interested in science?" you may be able to recycle that entire essay you wrote earlier and save valuable time.

3. Use different parts of past personal statements or essays to create entirely new essays. (Remember that a few paragraphs from old essays with a few new sentences added to them creates an entirely new essay.)

4. Ask your recommenders if you can have multiple copies of their recommendations. If they agree to give you multiple copies, make sure each recommendation copy has their signature on it or is in a signed envelope (if needed).

5. Always have extra copies of your résumé, standardized test scores (ACT, SAT), and FAFSA Student Aid Report (SAR). You will definitely need these items the majority of time when applying for scholarships. Having copies ready saves you valuable time.

6. Keep an electronic copy of all of your scholarship essays/ personal statements, and résumés on a flash drive. This will keep you prepared to take advantage of any opportunities that come your way without notice.

MillionDollarScholar's Interviewing Attire Guidelines

Ladies:

1. For every interview, wear a pant/skirted suit, or a suit-like pants or skirt, with a professional blouse.

2. You may wear a blazer over the professional blouse that does not match the skirt or pant color.

3. Your suit color should be navy, dark grey, or any dark neutral shade.

4. If your suit or blazer is solid, try to wear a patterned blouse. If your suit or blazer is patterned, wear a solid blouse. These combinations complement each other.

5. Skirts should not sit above the knee.

6. Pantyhose should not have any runs and should be conservative in color.

7. Makeup should be minimal and accentuate natural skin tones. Do not apply extreme colors.

8. You hair should be styled professionally, and you should not apply too much perfume.

Gentlemen:

1. Try your best to wear a suit to every interview.

2. If you do not have a suit, wear pressed khakis or slacks with a blazer or suit jacket of some kind over your dress shirt. If you do not have a blazer, just wear your dress shirt and slacks.

3. Your suit color should be navy or dark grey (charcoal).

4. Your dress shoes should be either black or dark brown. Make sure that your belt color matches your shoe color.

5. You can never go wrong with a solid white dress shirt.

6. No matter what color shirt you are wearing, if it is a solid shirt, wear a patterned tie. This can be polka dots, stripes, gingham, checks, boxes, paisley, or plaid. If your shirt is patterned, wear a solid tie. These are called *shirt and tie combinations*, and having a complementary combination screams WINNER!

7. Grooming is also a part of your attire, so make sure that your head and facial hair are neat and groomed. Do not put on too much cologne.

MillionDollarScholar's General Interviewing Rules

1. Practice interviewing in the mirror two days and the day before your interview. Do not be afraid to literally ask yourself questions in the mirror and respond out loud to them. This will help you gather some potential talking points for the interview, reduce your anxiety or nervousness, and find your best interview voice. It may feel a little crazy asking yourself questions and responding to them, but you would much rather look crazy in a room by yourself than to look unprepared in a real scholarship interview. Trust me.

2. Develop one or two really good questions that you would like to ask the interviewers at the end of the interview. These questions should clearly show that you have thought about the interview beforehand and that you are genuinely interested in the people interviewing you.

3. Your dress should always be business causal. While this is the time to put on the best clothes in your closet, make sure that your attire makes a statement while still being subtle.

4. Always show up fifteen to twenty minutes early for an interview.

5. Turn your cellular phone on silent mode or off. This means it should not even vibrate during the interview.

6. Never check your phone during an interview. That message or call can wait!

7. Do not fidget your fingers or give attention to other items such as a pen while the interviewers are speaking.

8. Be confident in all your answers; you made it far enough to get the interview, so give responses that show the interviewers that you deserve the.

9. Never leave the interview without showing appreciation to the interviewer(s) by saying "thank you" and that you look forward to communication in the future.

CONNECT With MILLIONDOLLARSCHOLAR

Want updated information on The Scholarship Race and continued access to valuable scholarship resources?

- Connect on Facebook to find out about any speaking engagements/workshops near you in the future. Learn about current scholarship, internship, and professional opportunities for high school and college students.
- Connect via e-mail to ask a question about scholarships and to give book feedback.
- Use the upcoming MillionDollar$cholar website to download the MD$ Scholarship Pyramid™, the MD$ Scholarship Table™ Worksheet, activity résumé templates, and much more.

Facebook

www.facebook.com/milliondollarscholar

E-mail

info@milliondollarscholar.com

Website

www.milliondollarscholar.com *(Coming Soon)*